Frankie Moffatt was born in Coleraine, Northern Ireland in 1953 and attended Millburn Primary School, Coleraine Academical Institution and Dalriada School Ballymoney. After starting work, he continued his education on a part time basis at Jordanstown Polytechnic and the University of Ulster in Coleraine.

After spending a lifetime in business, specialising in the field of Procurement and Supply Chain Management, retirement accompanied by lockdown due to the COVID-19 pandemic afforded him the time and opportunity to fulfil a lifetime ambition to write a book and *The Penzance Smash* is the result of these efforts.

He now lives very happily in the beautiful North Coast town of Portstewart with his wife Anne, with his three daughters and five grandchildren living nearby.

This book is dedicated to the memory of my late father, Joe. This man brought me and my brother up on his own after the tragic death of our mother when we were very young and without him, we would not be the people we are today. We can never repay him for all that he gave us.

It is also dedicated to the memory of my late mother, Minnie. Although our time together was short, her influence, gentle ways and love have never been forgotten.

It is dedicated to my big brother, Adrian, who also lived this story and who I look up to, to this day.

Finally, it is dedicated to my wife, Anne, the love of my life; our four children, the first unfortunately born asleep but never forgotten, followed by Zara, Laura and Ruth and our five grandchildren Jon, Sara, Joe, Ben and Alex.

Frankie Moffatt

THE PENZANCE SMASH

A story of one loft, one race
and one family

AUSTIN MACAULEY PUBLISHERS™

LONDON • CAMBRIDGE • NEW YORK • SHARJAH

A CIP catalogue record for this title is available from the British Library.

ISBN 9781398457324 (Paperback)
ISBN 9781398458178 (ePub e-book)

www.austinmacauley.com

First Published 2021
Austin Macauley Publishers Ltd®
1 Canada Square
Canary Wharf
London
E14 5AA

Firstly, I would like to thank Mark Roughan for his wonderful and endless support on this project. Without him, this book would probably never have come to life. His advice and critique of the manuscript has proven to not only be insightful but also invaluable.

Secondly, to Kimberly Hartnett Marlow, the professional in all of this. Kimberly has been the guiding hand providing expert advice and support throughout the process. I thank her for treating the work sensitively, never changing it with her editing, taking the book to another level and I can never thank her enough for that.

My thanks also go to my wife Anne and daughters Zara, Laura and Ruth for their support and keeping me on track. This book is for you.

The Penzance Smash

Introduction

This short story is best described using the words of the great American singer-songwriter, Kris Kristofferson. It is partly truth and partly fiction.

Whilst some of the pigeon names and details have been changed, it is based on true life events. It is a family history of sorts, telling of real people and of a sport which, once extremely popular, has now, sadly, almost disappeared.

It tells of working-class people who took great care of, and pride in, their families, their homing pigeons, and who also displayed exceptional levels of sportsmanship.

This pastime they shared was not about money – as there was not much. It was about caring for their birds, racing them, and trying to create a bloodline suitable for certain types of races. The sport is full of stories of great love, dedication, and bravery, of never giving up, and overcoming the harshest conditions the elements can throw at you. In many ways, it mirrors life itself.

What follows is a story of one loft, one race and one family.

Frankie Moffatt

The Loft

Joe Moffatt had been breeding and racing homing pigeons since he was just a little boy. It was a hobby inherited from his father and it fascinated him. He was keenly interested in birds bred to fly long distances and loved to hear the older fanciers tell stories of their prized birds flying home from such far-off places as Penzance, on the south coast of England, and from various locations in France such as St. Malo, Avranches, and Les Sables.

Joe and his young wife, Minnie, set up a home in the newly built Milburn Housing Estate which became known simply as the Calf Lane to all who lived there. In the early 1950s, they had two sons, Adrian and Frankie, and Joe worked hard as a painter and decorator to provide for his family. In his spare time, he pursued his passion, building a loft in the back garden for his team of prized pigeons.

Joe's pride and joy was a Blue Bard cock called Proud Boy. Oh, he loved that pigeon! He raised him from a chick, and it was evident to all that they had a great bond. Proud Boy would come when called and perch on Joe's shoulder. They would chat to each other and plan the strategy for forthcoming races together. He had successfully flown France four times – a remarkable feat for any pigeon – and Joe was now carefully planning for him to take it easier and to move on to the next stage of his life.

Joe called the pigeon to him. "Well, old boy, the time has finally come for you to stop racing," he said gently.

Proud Boy was shocked. He was born to race. He loved being the top bird in the loft. He shook his light grey head. "No! Why would you want me to stop?"

"I know you don't like it," said Joe, "but I want to keep you safe as you have a more important job to do for me now."

"What can be more important than flying and winning races?" asked Proud Boy indignantly.

This old boy's racing record was second to none and Joe often marvelled over how one bird could have done it. Proud Boy first flew France in 1958 from St. Malo, a distance of 490 miles, being first home in the club with a time of almost 12 hours. In 1960, he repeated the feat, again winning club honours, this time taking 14 hours to cover the distance in the very harshest of conditions.

In 1961, these successes prompted Joe to target the most prestigious race of all, the King's Cup from Les Sables, a distance of 620 miles which was entered by fanciers from all over the island of Ireland. This race turned out to be a disaster with only 32 birds making it home in the allotted race time of three days. Proud Boy struggled home on the ninth day, exhausted and covered in oil. This bird just didn't know how to give up.

The next year, Joe again set his sights on the King's Cup, but at the last moment changed his mind and switched Proud Boy to the shorter race from St. Malo. He felt the extra distance from Les Sables would make it practically impossible for him to beat birds from down the country. This turned out to be a terrible decision. The race was an even bigger disaster than Les Sables had been the year before, with only nine birds home in the three days' race time. Proud Boy again didn't give up and bravely battled home on the fifth day!

The warrior had done it again. Now, Joe had decided that he was home to stay.

"I am so proud of you," Joe said to Proud Boy. "You are so brave! But you are getting older, and I need you to sire the next generation of birds. It is vitally important to build on your bloodline to ensure the future success of this loft."

Proud Boy realized the wisdom in Joe's words. He knew in his heart of hearts that he was finding each race more difficult and often arrived home totally exhausted. With a heavy heart, he accepted that his flying days were ending. He nuzzled into Joe's neck for comfort and reassurance.

"It will be OK, you'll see," Joe whispered. "It is the right decision, and the timing is right. You'll soon have youngsters and I need you to pass on all your knowledge to them on strategy and tactics, and more importantly, on how to stay safe."

Proud Boy sighed and Joe knew he would have to give the bird a little more time to come to terms with things. He gently lifted the bird off his shoulder and put him on his perch in the loft for the night.

"Good night old boy, sleep well," said Joe. "We'll talk more in the morning."

There was not much sleep that night in Maple Drive. Both Joe and Proud Boy were restless as they thought about the changes coming.

Joe rose earlier than usual and went about his normal chores of feeding and watering all the birds in the loft and letting them out for a little exercise. He called Proud Boy to him, "Come on, come on, old boy!"

The bird understood this call well and swooped down and settled beside Joe. He was anxious to hear more.

Joe began to explain the second and critically important part of the plan. "I have spent several months now looking for a partner for you," he said. "I've found exactly what I am looking for in Belgium. She is a great little pigeon, a Delbar, bred like you and her ancestors before her, to fly long distances. You will make a perfect pair and I am sure your chicks will go on to be great racing pigeons."

Proud Boy liked this idea of this fancy Flemish bird as his partner. He was also impressed that she shared his heritage. It was beginning to sound like a match made in heaven.

"She's of royal blood, and is called 'Princess Sofia'," Joe continued. "Her family have a great racing tradition. She will be arriving in a couple of days, so you will need to let everyone else know she is coming and prepare a comfortable nest box for you and her to live in."

Proud Boy happily set about these tasks and like everyone else, he could not wait for the arrival of their new loft mate. The other hens in the loft excitedly chatted amongst themselves.

"I wonder if she's beautiful?"

"Do you think she can speak English?"

"I hear she is a royal, I hope she isn't snobbish and thinks that she can rule the roost!"

All of their questions were answered when the big day finally arrived. She was indeed very beautiful, a small, checkered hen with white markings and a sassy walk. Proud Boy was immediately smitten. It was love at first sight.

13

She spoke English with a funny little accent and sent Proud Boy's heart a-flutter every time she spoke. The other hens laughed and tried, in fun, to mimic her, but it has to be said, without too much success. She was certainly not a snob and when first introduced told everyone, "Just call me Sofi, and I am pleased to meet you all!"

Sofi seemed a bit shy but was quietly confident. The other birds in the loft quickly accepted her and liked to spend time listening to stories of her homeland and her family back in Belgium. They admired her sophistication and dreamt of being like her.

She never told Proud Boy what she thought when she first saw him, as even thinking it made her blush. "Oh my, my! What a handsome bird," she thought. "Everything a girl could wish for!" She thought he looked dashing as he was, by far, the tallest bird in the loft, had a deep barrel chest with feathers of beautiful purple and mauve hues. His strong wings were light grey with two perfect dark stripes.

Joe watched and waited for the two to become acquainted. After a few weeks, he was pleased that Sofi had settled in so well and that his master plan was coming together. The two pigeons were inseparable, flying together when out for exercise and sitting in their nest box chatting long into the night. Joe was happy to see Proud Boy so content. He had obviously come to terms with this change in his life.

The Girls

A few months passed and it became evident to Joe that there would soon be the fluttering of little wings about the loft. He and Proud Boy kept a careful watch and were delighted when Sofi proudly showed them her two eggs. Proud Boy fussed about her and took his turn to sit on the eggs to keep them warm. After four weeks the eggs hatched, and two beautiful little chicks were born. Proud Boy strutted around the loft with his chest puffed out and his head held high, telling everyone about the new arrivals.

He and Sofi, like all expectant parents, had spent many hours thinking of names for their children. They wanted the names to continue family traditions and to also denote their status. It was therefore decided that the children, both girls, would be called Proud Girl and Princess Elisabeth.

This was a very busy time in the loft as the other hens were also having their chicks. Joe had to be on his toes to make sure all were well. There were a total of 12 chicks hatched that season and to everyone's relief, all turned out to be fit and healthy.

The youngsters were having the time of their lives, happily playing together. The loft was filled with joy and laughter from morning to night. The girls, as Proud Boy called his daughters, were full of life. They got up to all sorts of mischief, often ending up under their mother's wings, being gently scolded. Sofi was very loving with soft nature and could just not bear to shout at them. Instead, she would softly chide them, calling them 'my hearts' in Flemish.

"Mijn lief, you must behave, otherwise, your Pa will be disappointed and angry," Sofi would say. "Now, you don't want that, do you?"

The girls would solemnly shake their heads. "No Moeke, we will try to be good!"

Sofi would give them a big hug and send them on their way.

Proud Boy would watch this from a distance and smile. He thought the girls got up to so much mischief because they loved being brought under their mother's wings for the hugs and that they did not see it in any way as punishment.

The young birds loved the evenings in the loft when they gathered around for story time. They sat enthralled as the older pigeons told stories of the races they had flown and the trophies they had won. They particularly liked the stories told by Proud Boy and by a much-respected bird called Warhorse. Both told thrilling tales of flying long distances along different routes from France. When the youngsters went to bed, they dreamt of making such heroic journeys themselves.

Important Lessons

As for all children, there comes a time when the serious business of going to school must start. This is very important in a pigeon loft with subjects such as Etiquette, History and Geography at the top of the list, but with the topic of Safety taking precedence over everything else.

Their teacher was that formidable old bird, Warhorse, who had been appointed Health and Safety Officer for the loft. This extremely important position involved educating the young birds on all the dangers that lay outside the confines of the loft, as well as conducting weekly Risk Assessments and Safety Audits to ensure there were no holes or gaps in the loft which predators such as foxes or cats could get through and attack the pigeons. Long ago, Warhorse had seen the devastation that followed a cat getting into a loft, and he was determined such a thing would never happen on his watch. He was also responsible for inspecting the traps, the landing boards that led the birds back into the loft, making sure they were in perfect working order for race days.

Before the young birds were allowed out to circle with their parents, they had to be made aware of the dangers that faced them. Warhorse warned them of the risk of flying into electric wires or telephone lines, especially in low light, such as dusk. More homes were having telephones installed and the threat of hard-to-see phone lines was increasing, he warned. Warhorse stressed the need for the young birds to watch and learn from their parents, in particular, to focus and concentrate when circling, especially at lower heights.

He taught them how to identify hawks and cats and to stay clear of those predators. "Even if you see just one of these, get to the loft as fast as you can," he warned the youngsters. It was only when Warhorse felt that all the young birds fully understood the risks and had passed their Safety Exam that he allowed them to go out on the wing with their parents.

They all respected Warhorse, even as they joked among themselves about his funny accent and appearance. He had a strong Scottish brogue and wore a kilt which appeared to be struggling to stay up under the weight of his ever-expanding belly. He carried a cane under his wing and used it as a pointer when conducting lessons on the blackboard. He also threatened to use it on them if they did not pay attention, although no one could recall an occasion when he made good on this threat.

The first flights with their parents were big milestones for the young birds. They were very happy and excited. Before his daughters made their first such flights, Proud Boy sat them down for some stern directions. "Now girls, remember everything you were taught in class and stay close to me and Mummy," he said. "Listen and learn as we will show you where all the wires are located and explain how high you must fly to avoid them."

The girls lined up behind their mummy and daddy and before going out of the traps. Proud Boy turned to them and gave them a final warning, "No messing about out here, okay?" The girls nodded their agreement.

Off they went. The girls were exhilarated as they circled beside their parents. They listened intently as the locations of all the wires were pointed out. After a brief time, they returned to the loft, exhausted.

Day by day, they flew for longer periods, becoming stronger and more confident on the wing until the time finally came when all the young birds were allowed out without their parents. They loved this free time chasing each other. A favourite of the girls was a game called Kiss Catch in which the boys had chances to steal quick pecks. They thought this was so naughty! It was great fun.

The young birds went to school each day for their other lessons. Sofi had been a teacher at home in Belgium, so she took on the role of educating the youngsters in what she referred to as Etiquette, which Proud Boy privately thought was just a fancier foreign word for good manners.

They were taught History and learnt that they were one of the oldest domesticated birds alive, used in early Egyptian and Roman times for entertainment and to carry messages. Proud Girl and Princess Elisabeth were fascinated to learn of the huge popularity of pigeon racing in Belgium in the mid-19th century when the fanciers bred pigeons, especially for speed and endurance. These birds, called Voyageurs, were their ancestors, which made the girls very proud of their heritage.

They learnt about the Voyageurs' great strength and speed that led to homing pigeons playing important roles in both World Wars. Thousands of the birds carried messages back to base from behind enemy lines. The heroics of these birds excited all the youngsters and made them feel very special. They realized that they had a great tradition to uphold and vowed to do so at every opportunity.

Geography was also very important, and they were taught about the position of their loft to the others. They learnt about the location and distances of the places from which they would fly. Training tosses are a very important activity in the development of a young racing pigeon as they are first educated in the fact that they have a homing instinct which is governed by the earth's magnetic forces. They are then all put into baskets together and taken to locations of ever-increasing distances and released to fly home. This is designed to not only build their strength but also their confidence in their homing instinct. They learnt how to fly in different conditions and develop a natural flight path back to their loft based on the direction of the wind.

Joe loved to watch the young birds circling and playing around the loft. His oldest son, Adrian, was taking an interest in the birds and joined him more and more often. The same could not be said of the younger boy, Frankie, who was only interested in chasing after a ball or fishing for newts in the Quarry!

"It will soon be time for the young birds to finish their schooling and to begin race training," Joe said to 11-year-old Adrian. "How do you feel about helping me with this batch of youngsters?" Adrian was delighted and he immediately agreed.

"You know this will be hard work," said Joe. "It will mean getting up early in the morning to take the birds to the station for their training tosses, feeding them and cleaning the loft out every night." This did not put Adrian off, as he was beginning to love being about the birds and learning from his dad.

When Frankie heard about this, he was aghast. "Are you mad?" he asked his brother. "Doing all that and then having to clean the loft – there is no way I am doing that!"

Joe and Adrian just laughed. Over time Frankie grew to understand the love his father and brother shared for the sport but he never changed his opinion about cleaning out a loft!

At this time, pigeon racing was very much a sport of the working class. No fewer than six other fanciers had lofts near Joe's in the Calf Lane. There was Jim Maguire, Joe's brother, Willie; Johnnie McCandless, Louis Thompson, Jim 'Sainty' Gamble and Jerry Donaghy. They were all great friends and came to Joe's house on a Sunday evening in their own unofficial little pigeon club. Often, fanciers from other parts of the town would join them and they would have great craic talking all things pigeon. A regular visitor was Wee Joe Magee from Killowen, and he would entertain the others by singing old Irish ballads in his wonderful tenor voice.

Adrian loved to sit on the floor listening and learning from these great fanciers. Frankie, however, found it boring and was even amused that they thought they could tell which pigeons would make good racers by looking at their eyeballs with a magnifying glass.

"Can you imagine it?" Frankie would think to himself. *"They call it 'eye sign' – they're all mad!"* However, these men were generous and gifted. If one man had a good pigeon, he would breed it and give one of the offspring to another, hoping they too would have success with a strong racer.

Having so many other lofts nearby was great fun for the young birds in Joe's loft and they made many friends when out flying. Proud Girl and Princess Elisabeth loved to catch the eyes of the boys from the other lofts and flirt with them. They chittered away to each other.

"Oh, isn't he cool!" or "I saw him first!"

Then they would swoop up into the air in a fit of laughter.

Proud Boy and Sofi were delighted to see their girls having so much fun in the days before their race training would start in earnest.

Training to Race

It was in early April that Joe called Proud Boy to him and told him to prepare the young birds for their first training toss in the coming week. Proud Boy quickly got to work and called a team meeting for all the birds the next morning. He called them to order at 10 a.m. on the dot.

"Okay, everyone! Joe has decided that the first training toss is to be next week, and it is to be from the Two-Mile Bridge. For you youngsters, this is the beginning of the important work to prepare you for your racing career."

All of the young birds started chatting excitedly and Proud Boy clapped his wings loudly. "Quiet! Listen carefully! First thing every morning you will attend a Health and Safety Refresher Course with Warhorse to remind you of the dangers that lie out there."

This was met by a collective groan. Proud Boy pushed on. "There will be no excuses or exceptions and anyone missing a class will not be allowed to take part in the first toss."

This got their attention.

"Your safety comes first but it is important for you to learn to fly from greater distances where you cannot see the home loft," Proud Boy explained. "You know, you have a homing instinct and now is the time to use it."

After the meeting broke up, the young birds could talk about nothing else for the next few days. Even Proud Girl and Princess Elisabeth were distracted from their thoughts of chasing boys and started to focus on the tasks ahead.

Sofi sat with them and quietly reminded them of their great heritage. "Mijn Liefs, remember you are Voyageurs and are of Belgian Royal Blood. You are also the daughters of Proud Boy and everyone in this loft will be looking to you to do well. Those from other lofts will see you as competition that they have to beat. You must now focus and rise to the challenge. I am your Moeke, and I know, if you concentrate and work hard, you can do it."

The girls loved their mother very much and vowed to each other that they would do everything they could to make her proud.

They, like the other youngsters in the loft, did what they were told and attended the Health and Safety Refresher classes every morning. They rested and ate well, cutting out junk food, building up their strength for the first training toss.

Meanwhile, Joe had been spending a lot of time with Adrian, setting out the schedule for the training of this year's youngsters. One evening, they were sitting together having a cup of tea, which was something Joe loved (along with the ever-present cigarette). He knew he needed to prepare the young boy not only for the great things about the sport but also for those things that were not so nice. "You know Son, this is a great hobby, but it will be very upsetting if any of the birds get injured – or worse, killed or lost."

Adrian answered, "I know Da, but I want to do it. I like working with the pigeons." As he said the words, Adrian realised he was speaking more out of bravado than real confidence. He had not thought about birds being lost or killed.

Joe continued, explaining to his son that there was an old saying in pigeon racing: "You have to be cruel to be kind." Adrian nodded, but little did he know that there would be many times in the years to come when he would face this truth. He would learn that it is best to put a mortally injured or seriously ill pigeon to sleep to save it from pain or to prevent the spread of disease. All fanciers have to face these difficult decisions and learn to live with the consequences.

Joe moved on to the tasks they needed to accomplish. "Right, Son, the next thing we have to do is ring the birds. Each bird must have a metal ring with a number put onto its leg which can never be removed. This is what is known as their Life Ring. The owner, the name of the bird and this number are then registered with the National Union of Racing Pigeons before it can race. This becomes its unique identifier and also helps to trace it back to its home loft if it gets lost."

Adrian had, of course, noticed the Life Rings on their birds, but hadn't realized all that was involved. He nodded in understanding when Joe went on to explain how the rings helped prevent cheating during races.

The next morning, Sunday, was a day of rest for the birds and they normally enjoyed a wee lie in. However, this morning the loft was buzzing with activity as all the parents prepared their youngsters to receive their Life Rings. This was an important rite of passage for the young pigeons. They had to look their very best: bathed, preened, and with feathers shining to perfection.

Proud Girl and Princess Elisabeth were very excited and scurrying about in front of the mirror admiring themselves.

"Moeke, Moeke, are my tail feathers clean?"

"What about mine? What about mine?"

"I hope I get a nice Life Ring number!"

"I hope I get one I can remember!"

Sofi smiled and quietly said in her beautiful accent, "Calm down, you both look very beautiful. Now sit at peace as it will soon be time and I don't want you to get your feathers all ruffled."

Joe and Adrian had set up a little table in the loft for the Ringing Ceremony. Proud Boy and Princess Sofia, using her full title in the loft for the first time in recognition of the importance of the occasion, were extremely happy as they led the girls forward and presented them to Joe and Adrian to receive their rings. The girls were in their element, strutting and wiggling their tail feathers.

"What a fine-looking pair we have here!" said Joe with a laugh, making the girls giggle.

He turned to the parents. "You have done a great job. You should both be very proud," he said.

Proud Boy and Sofi were delighted and hugged each other as the girls received their rings.

Joe had also a special message for the girls. "I expect a lot of you two young ladies and Adrian is going to be your trainer," he whispered to them. "He will be good to you so make sure you do your best for him. Now, off you go and have lots of fun today."

The girls were happy with this news as they liked Adrian and were looking forward to the day ahead.

All of the parents, in turn, proudly brought their youngsters forward to receive their rings and Joe had kind words of encouragement for all of them. He and Adrian had also laid on a special banquet of their favourite foods and the birds had a great time, singing and dancing into the early evening when they retired for the night. They knew they would need to be up early the next morning.

As usual, the girls were chittering away in bed and Proud Boy had to tell them: "Get to sleep, girls! You'll need all your energy tomorrow."

They soon settled down and slipped off to sleep, for once, not dreaming of boys but trying to memorise their ring numbers by repeating them over and over in their heads. This proved to be better than counting sheep!

A Big Day

Joe and Adrian were up at first light and out to the loft to catch the birds and put them in the basket ready to go to the station to catch the first train to Belfast at 6:30 a.m.

"Go gently, Son," Joe reminded Adrian. "You don't want to hurt them or damage their wings as you put them into the basket."

It was no easy task to catch a dozen excited young birds and it took longer than usual because Adrian was being so careful. Joe knew things would quicken up in the days to come. They rushed up to the station with Adrian insisting on carrying the basket despite it getting heavier with every step. Joe smiled to himself, knowing his son was taking his duties very seriously. They made it just on time and got the basket safely loaded onboard minutes before the train set off.

The train conductor had an important job in this process. He knew all the pigeon fanciers and would stop the train at the designated spots, unload the baskets, and release the pigeons to fly home. He would then load up the empty baskets and the train would continue with its human passengers to its final destination.

Meanwhile, Joe and Adrian rushed back home to wait for the birds to arrive.

Proud Boy and Warhorse had also left the loft early, flying out to Two Mile Bridge, circling, and waiting for the train to arrive and the youngsters to be released. Their role was to watch and guide any young birds home that seemed to be struggling.

However, it appeared that they were not needed as this batch of youngsters quickly took to the skies and immediately headed off in the right direction. It was a southerly wind which meant it was in their tails and they flew home at a great speed. Proud Girl and Princess Elisabeth were at the head of the team and were loving it, changing the lead many times, laughing merrily as they did so.

Joe and Adrian took up their positions at the scullery window which gave them a perfect view of the direction the birds were to come from. After a short wait, Joe pointed in the distance, saying, "Here they come!" Adrian looked but could see nothing. Joe smiled and kept pointing. Soon Adrian could make out the shapes of the pigeons as they approached the loft. Over time he would learn, like Joe, to spot them when they were only pinpricks in the sky and identify them. (Frankie marvelled at this skill. He could only ever see them when they were practically landing on the traps, much to the amusement of the other two.)

"Come on, Son," said Joe, "let's get out and get settled before they land. It's important that there are no distractions to stop them trapping." He wanted Adrian to understand that races could be won or lost in the few seconds it took for the birds to get into the traps. Indeed, neighbours of the fanciers in the Calf Lane were so understanding of this that they didn't hang out washing on the clothesline in the garden on race days to avoid possibly scaring the birds as they flapped about in the wind.

Joe picked up a tin filled with a mixture of beans and corn on their way out to the loft. As the youngsters began arriving, Joe rattled the tin, calling, "Come on, come on" to lure them inside the loft as quickly as possible.

But instead of going straight inside, some of the youngsters landed on the roof or circled about in excitement. Proud Boy and Warhorse saw this and went to work, shooing them and telling them they had to trap and eat something before they would be allowed out to play again. They knew it was so important for the young birds to learn this and would talk to them about it later.

Once all the birds were successfully trapped and fed, Joe set off to work and Adrian headed to school, realizing that his normal day was just starting! He also had to call at the train station after school to collect the empty basket and to make it ready for the next training toss. It was a long day, but he enjoyed it. When he went to bed that night, he was sound asleep in seconds!

Progress...and Loss

This became the routine every other day for the next six weeks with the youngsters being dropped off farther and farther from home. The young birds were all getting stronger and quicker. Joe was impressed by the speed of the girls as they were generally first home, closely followed by the rest of the team. He thought this was a good sign as it showed all the birds were capable of travelling at fast speeds over long distances.

Well, almost all of them. There was one big boy, a Red, who was a bit of a straggler and always arrived home last. As this pattern developed the other youngsters would playfully tease him as they passed him. "Come on, Slowcoach," they shouted, or "See you tomorrow!" The bird took all of this in good spirits. He was a jolly big fella who even liked his nickname – Bootsy – that was given to him by his friends who joked that he needed boots to protect his feet from blisters when walking home.

The girls loved spending time with Bootsy, who was a happy-go-lucky friend to them. They always sought him out when they needed to be cheered up. Little did they know then that he would go on to play a major part in their lives.

Joe, Adrian, and Proud Boy could hear the friendly banter and it made them laugh. Yet, they all admired Bootsy immensely as he never gave up and made it home every time as quickly as he could. In their book, this was all you could ask of any pigeon!

During these training tosses, the youngsters learnt that when the wind was from the north and blowing into their faces, it was best to fly lower where there was more protection from the strong gusts. This would prove to be very valuable knowledge for them as they would often face such conditions when racing.

All was going well until the last training toss.

Just after they were released, the weather turned nasty. The sky turned black and heavy rain broke out accompanied by a biting north wind. Joe and Adrian were very concerned as they watched the birds return more slowly and more spread out in their number. Proud Boy was also anxious. A strange silence came over the loft as time passed and the youngsters were slowly being counted home.

6...7...8...9...10. And then, they stopped coming.

The clock continued ticking but there were no further arrivals. As time wore on and the light disappeared, the realization dawned that there was now a big problem. Panic spread as Warhorse confirmed that two were now officially missing. Their parents were distraught and all the other birds in the loft came round to comfort and reassure them.

"What do you think?" a worried Adrian asked his father. "Will they be okay? Will they get back in the morning?" Joe thought he knew the answers to those questions, but he did not reply as he did not want to upset his son before bed. A silent all-night vigil was held by Joe and the birds in the loft while Adrian quietly cried himself to sleep, fearing the worst. (Frankie slept, oblivious to it all, dreaming of scoring a goal in the Irish Cup Final for Coleraine.)

Morning came, then another, and another, with no good news. Everyone had to accept that the missing birds were gone forever. Did they just get lost? Were they safely living in another loft? Were they attacked and killed by hawks? Did they fly into electric or telephone lines? No one knew. A deep melancholy descended upon the loft and the girls were extremely upset. It was the first time they had experienced such loss. They were grieving and missing their two friends. They felt their hearts were going to break and their mother cuddled and reassured them.

"Mijn Liefs, unfortunately, this is part of growing up," she told them. "Perhaps you now understand the risks you will face every time you go out and why you have to concentrate and look after each other." The girls huddled even closer to their mother hoping she could take the pain away.

Proud Boy knew from experience that the only thing that could lift this mood was for there to be something else to focus on and he was glad that the first race was fast approaching. He and Warhorse set about getting the youngsters ready, but he knew that this sadness was something that would remain with all of them for the rest of their lives.

The Races Begin

Joe, Adrian, and Proud Boy had agreed on a race strategy. Proud Boy announced that the remaining 10 youngsters would be split into two teams of five. They were to race alternate weeks using the same release points. This meant they would all get the same amount of racing and experience but would be able to rest every other week. This would allow them to save their strength for later on in the season when they would have to fly much greater distances.

The original plan was for Proud Girl and Princess Elisabeth to split up and take leadership roles within each team. This plan changed after Proud Boy told Sofi who was instantly apoplectic. He had never seen her like this. "They must never be split up!" Sofi cried. "They must always fly together and look after each other!" She continued without taking a breath. "What if something happens to one of them and the other is not there to help? This cannot happen, I will not permit it!" She continued to shout, now breaking into frantic Flemish, and Proud Boy could not understand a word – but he knew it was not good. He went back to Joe and Adrian to explain the situation. Thankfully, they understood and accepted the plan that the girls would fly together. He was deeply relieved, as he certainly did not want to have to face Sofi again while she was this upset!

With Sofi pacified, Warhorse printed a copy of this season's race programme and posted a copy in the loft in a cellophane cover to protect it from damage. By now, the younger birds had come to understand and appreciate the older bird. At first, he had seemed like a grumpy taskmaster. But as they listened to their elders' stories, they learnt he had been in the army as a young bird, serving as a messenger during the Second World War. They loved to listen to stories of his flights through bombs and bullets as he carried messages back from behind enemy lines. They were in awe of his bravery and grew to understand his need for routine, rules, and military precision. They also understood why Joe had appointed him to the very important role of teaching them how to get home safely.

The race programme that Warhorse posted created great interest and read as follows:

Sutton 1
Sutton 2
Arklow 1
Arklow 2
Wexford 1
Wexford 2
Haverford West 1
Haverford West 2
Penzance

For the older birds, the list would continue to locations in France such as St. Malo or Avranches, followed by Les Sables. These were considered to be the ultimate challenges due to the distance and the fact that the birds would have to cover two stretches of water to make it home.

Pigeons typically do not like to fly over water as they know they cannot land on it if they are tired. They will often spend time flying up and down a coast trying to find a land crossing rather than face the water, exhausting themselves in the process. Many never attempt to cross and are, therefore, lost. Others that cross can perish in the dark choppy waters as they are just too tired to continue.

The girls were excited but apprehensive. This would be their first time in a proper race, competing with birds from other lofts. They knew they were the quickest in Joe's loft but did not know how they would fare against others from all around the country. Their days were spent going to classes with Warhorse, who reminded them of the risks they would face and finished every session with the same wise words: "Remember...above all, be safe out there."

Proud Boy educated them in the rules of racing. They would first be taken to the Club House where their details would be registered, and a rubber race ring would be placed on a leg. The number on this rubber ring would be matched to the number on their metal ring and recorded in the race book. This was to prevent cheating. When they arrived home, this rubber ring would be removed and put into a metal shuttle which would then be inserted into a specially designed race clock. The fancier would turn a wheel and the shuttle would be locked inside the clock and the time would be printed on special recording paper.

In the evening, after the race was completed, the fanciers took their clocks to the Club House, where the keys were kept. The clocks were opened by committee members who acted as impartial witnesses. They checked the rubber ring numbers against their race register and when satisfied that everything was alright, they removed the recording paper. Then each bird was 'clocked', meaning that the time and distance travelled were used to calculate the velocity or the speed of the flight. The bird with the quickest velocity was announced the winner. This was deemed to be the best way to even the playing field, although it was an imperfect method. The birds flying longer distances would always be more tired by the effort, yet longer distances were not factored into final results.

Proud Boy told them that on race day they would be transferred from their basket into larger cages in a conveyor, which was a vehicle designed to carry pigeons to the race point and then efficiently release them. He knew that this process could go wrong and had seen birds crushed and badly hurt in the rush. So, he carefully taught them how to position themselves in the cages to avoid injury. Once out of the cages, he said, "Fly as straight as you can for as long as you can and then swoop up as high as you can."

He had other important techniques for them to remember:

"Do not just follow the crowd but take a minute to get your bearings and allow your instinct to guide you, then set course for home."

"Fly as fast as you can to get away from the crowd. A crowd will attract hawks who know their chances of securing a tasty meal are better within a group."

"Too often, birds go out too fast early in the race and quickly run out of steam. Don't make the mistake of chasing them and tiring yourself out. Instead, follow my golden rule for racing which I call the two Fs – focus and fly!"

On the Thursday night before the first race, Sofi made sure that they all sat down for dinner and spent time together. Indeed, this became the norm before any race. Sofi was always aware that something bad could happen to her darling girls, and that these meals could be the last time all four would spend together. She wanted to make them happy times, every time. Proud Boy and the girls grew to love these little dinners and spending precious time with Moeke.

On Friday afternoon, Joe and Adrian caught the team of five birds entered into the first race, including Proud Girl, Princess Elizabeth, Basher's Boy, Anne's Lass and Bootsy. They took the birds to the Club to be registered and once there, Adrian chatted to two of his friends who were also sons of fanciers, and they helped their dads with the birds. One was John McCandless, a tall lanky lad with ginger hair and the other was William "Winky" Donaghy, who was very small, with thick black hair. Over the next weeks, it became a common sight to see the three of them going over the Tip Head side by side, like doorsteps, carrying their baskets of precious cargo.

Frankie laughed when he saw them. "You three could start a Country and Western Band," he shouted. "Big Johnny, Ady and Wee Winky!" He was clever enough to run away before they could catch him.

The birds were all loaded into the conveyor, and this was a different experience for the girls. It made them very uncomfortable and nervous. The conveyor stopped at Pigeon Clubs in every town as they made their way down the country, with more birds added at each stop. The girls were used to travelling by train and enjoyed the clickety-clack sounds and the gentle rocking. This was very different. They were not used to being crushed together with so many strangers speaking with different accents, some of which they couldn't understand. Bootsy noticed that they were frightened and made his way over beside them and started to chat and tell jokes to try to take their minds off things. After a while, they nodded off to sleep.

The next morning, they were all rudely awakened by loud banging and clanging as the sides of the conveyor was opened and the troughs were filled with fresh water and food. The birds were all desperate with thirst which led to a mad scramble. Proud Girl and Princess Elisabeth were not prepared for this and were pushed and buffeted to different corners. When they finally got back to each other, they hugged each other, unsure of what else lay ahead.

Bootsy saw what was happening and got the girls together along with their other two loft mates. "This is chaos, and we need to stick close together," he told them. "Follow me and remember everything we have been taught."

They stayed together and as soon as the sides of the cage dropped, they were off. They scrambled out and flew as low as they could, for as long as they could. Their racing instincts kicked in and all five swooped up as high as they could at the same time. They could now see clear skies all around them and below were hundreds of disorientated birds flying in all directions.

"This way!" shouted Bootsy. He pointed north with his wing. They all set off for home.

"*Hmmm…*" thought Princess Elisabeth, "*perhaps there is more to this big boy than meets the eye.*"

The weather was good, there was a slight tailwind, and they were making good speed.

As they flew north, they saw some birds veer off and out of the batches they were flying in, and they realized that these birds came from lofts that were closer to the race point than theirs. Their confidence was growing as familiar landmarks came into view. They saw that there were several birds ahead of them. Proud Girl shouted to her sister, "Right, let's show them what we can do!" And off they went.

Meanwhile, back in Maple Drive, Joe and Adrian had taken up their perches at the scullery window. Proud Boy and Warhorse settled on the roof. They all scanned the skies for any sign of the birds. Suddenly, Joe pointed and yelled, "'There's one! It looks like it is Louis Thompson's or Johnnie McCandless's." This was quickly followed by a shout from Adrian. "There they are, Da! Look! It's the girls and they are coming together!"

Joe quickly made his way out to the loft and both birds were trapped quickly with Joe taking off their rubber race rings, putting them in the shuttle, and securing them in the clock to record the time of their arrival.

While Sofi fussed about her girls, hugging them, and checking to be sure they were okay, Joe, Adrian, Proud Boy, and Warhorse went back to their perches and only left when all five birds arrived home.

And, yes, you guessed it; Bootsy straggled in last, as usual, with everyone delighted to see him.

The Family

Joe, Adrian, and Frankie had their normal Saturday treat of a fish supper takeaway from the Astoria Café and Joe then got himself and Adrian ready to go to the Club to hear the race results.

Joe was a very quiet man of simple tastes and was devoted to bringing up his two boys after the unfortunate death of his young wife, Minnie. He was never overly strict with them but made sure they understood right from wrong. The boys, whilst not angelic by any means, never wanted to let him down.

Theirs was not a house full of shouting or fighting, in fact, the boys could not recall a time when their father had raised his voice to them. They were happy but knew they were different in that they had no mother to come home to. People would wonder how they coped with such loss, but it served to make them stronger and bring them closer together as a family. Sadness did not linger about the house.

When well-meaning people referred to them as 'wee orphans', it bothered Frankie. *We're not orphans, we have our dad,* he'd think. Remembering his mother and her hugs and kisses made him feel better, not sad. Both boys grew up knowing that their dad was a special man, and he, in turn, made sure they missed out on nothing important for their upbringing.

Joe ensured that from a very young age, the boys were independent. He taught them to cook, to wash and iron their clothes, and to get themselves off to school each morning when he went to work. They did the shopping mainly in Jimmy Taylor's on Railway Road where Joe had an account. Adrian and Frankie got what they needed throughout the week and Joe settled the account at the weekend after he got his wages. Sometimes, they shopped in Cameron's which was through the Arch on the Portrush Road.

Joe and Adrian favoured healthy food, especially the staple of the old Irish diet, potatoes, and fresh vegetables. Frankie, left to his own devices, preferred school dinners and at home, he loved cooked ham and Tayto cheese-and-onion crisp sandwiches. He also loved going to Granny and Granda's in Baptist Lane for Sunday dinner where his Granda, Big Joe, would always have a large pot of pea and ham soup for him. (Frankie loved that soup so much that he once ate such a lot that he landed in the hospital with stomach pains.)

Like the rest of their friends, their days were spent out in the fresh air, playing football on the green in front of their house. Frankie loved these games (or sides as they were called) and they often went on from morning to night. He ran about pretending he was Denis Law, the great inside forward from his favourite team, Manchester United. When he scored a goal, he would wheel away with one arm raised in the air clutching his cuff mimicking his hero's goal celebration. When not playing football, they fished for newts in the Quarry or spricks in the burn. Frankie normally returned from these expeditions soaked to the skin – if there was water about, he seemed destined to fall into it. They also spent a lot of time with their friends building huts up 'the hilly' or sliding down 'Superman's' using cardboard boxes as sledges.

It was a time when everyone looked out for each other. Doors were left open, and no one would dream of stealing from their neighbour. The Calf Lane was a great place to grow up – so much so that Adrian continues to live there, 60 years later.

Joe was never seen during the week in anything other than his white bibbed working overalls, covered in splashes of paint in all the colours of the rainbow, accompanied by his ever-present flat cap. He grew long sideburns and a horseshoe moustache. (The boys wondered where his love of this style came from. Frankie thought it might be from the Western movies, but who knows?)

Joe always dressed in his best clothes to go to the Club on a Saturday evening for the race results and then to the pub for a couple of drinks with some of the other fanciers. He was not a big drinker but did enjoy a beer sometimes followed by a whiskey or on special occasions, a wee brandy.

So it was that after the race, Joe, and Adrian, dressed in their best clothes, then set off for the Club. Joe could tell Adrian was nervous as he kept asking the same questions. "How do you think we have done? Do you think we won?" Joe didn't think so, but he kept giving his son the same calm answer. "Let's see when we get there, Son."

The Club was buzzing when they arrived. All the fanciers were chatting and asking how the others had done. Finally, the room was called to order, and they listened with bated breath as the results were readout.

In 1st Place...Frankie Telford

2nd...Sammy Wilson

3rd...Louis Thompson

4th...Moffatt Bros

5th...Moffatt Bros

Adrian never heard another word after this as he was thinking over and over to himself:

"4th and 5th...4th and 5th."

Joe didn't say anything but simply looked at the young boy and gave him a smile and a small nod of the head.

The boys knew that their father was a man of few words and not one to criticize nor lavish them with praise. Instead, they learnt that if he thought they had done well, he would make sure he could catch their eye, even across a crowded room, and give them a small nod of the head. Frankie thought of this as the 'Silent Nod of Approval' and it would come to mean more to him than all the money in the world.

After the results were all read out. the fanciers mingled, congratulating the winners, and chatting about how their birds had flown. Adrian was only interested in getting back to the loft to let the birds know the results. He said goodbye to his dad, rushed home and out to the loft. The birds had all been waiting, so they were excited when they saw him coming. He could hardly wait to tell them.

"Proud Girl, you were 4th and Princess Elisabeth was 5th. Basher's Boy; 11th, Anne's Lass; 23rd and...Bootsy 35th...but not last!" And everyone, including Bootsy, roared with laughter.

The girls went to bed early as they were exhausted and quickly fell into a deep sleep, leaving another big day in their lives behind them.

The next morning, Joe noticed Adrian was unusually quiet and asked him if anything was wrong. Adrian finally admitted he was a little disappointed that they hadn't won. It was then that he learnt one of the greatest lessons in his life. "Listen, Son," Joe said, "it is not all about winning, but more about taking part and doing your best. That is all you can ask of yourself or anyone else for that matter. Always remember to congratulate the winners but also recognize all who took part." He continued, "We were big winners yesterday as all the birds returned safe and sound. As a fancier, that is all you can hope for and anything else is a bonus."

These words resonated with the young boy, and he never forgot them.

As the season progressed, the two teams racing out of the loft continued to fly well with no injuries. Proud Girl and Princess Elisabeth were gaining confidence and coping better than they did in the first race. They continued to finish high in the placings.

Joe, Adrian, and Proud Boy would chat after each race, and they were pleased with what they were seeing from the youngsters. Joe was very encouraged as they were arriving home reasonably fresh, and he felt this was a good sign when thinking about the longer races to come.

He had always dreamt of winning the Young Bird Derby which was flown each year from Penzance in the south coast of England, a distance of some 350 miles. This was the Blue-Ribbon event of the young-bird racing calendar and Joe was secretly beginning to think he had a real chance with either of the two girls.

He also held a long and burning ambition of winning the Old Bird National from France but worried that it was too big an ask for a bird from the North Coast of Ireland. France was seen as the ultimate challenge for any bird and whilst Proud Boy had completed the remarkable feat of flying it four times, he found it impossible to beat the birds from down the country. He felt they had an unfair advantage as they did not have as far to fly. Joe thought it would be interesting to see how the girls would develop in the longer term and see if they could realistically take on this challenge. He couldn't help but hope.

A Sister to the Rescue

In the meantime, they decided to focus on the Young Bird Derby. They agreed that both Proud Girl and Princess Elisabeth had the speed and endurance necessary to win. They set about preparing them for the race. It was decided that the birds would be rested as much as possible to build up their strength and would only go out on short training tosses.

Their plans were thrown into complete disarray just two days before leaving for the race. The birds were out for some light exercise along with their friends. It was a beautiful day, and they were just messing about. They were not concentrating and did not see the pair of hawks hiding in the trees on the Ballymoney Line waiting to attack. The hawks were very cunning predators and had positioned themselves with the sun at their backs so that the glare blocked the view of the young pigeons until it was too late. The hawks attacked with rapier-like speed. The birds veered in all directions, trying to avoid the hawks, but Princess Elisabeth felt a sharp pain and a surge of panic, as a hawk's claw ripped through the skin of her throat.

"Everyone fly low and use the electric lines for cover!" shouted Bootsy.

Now, this command flew in the face of everything they had been taught, but the birds saw no other choice, so all quickly followed him down, flying for home below the lines. The hawks swooped a few more times but realized their chance had gone and so gave up the chase.

Princess Elisabeth was losing a lot of blood and her strength was evaporating quickly. Proud Girl saw what was happening. She flew alongside her sister and reassured her.

"You are going to be alright, the hawks are gone," she told her wounded sister. "I am going to fly just in front of you so grab my tail feathers and hold on. I won't leave you and I will get you home!"

It was all Princess Elisabeth could do to catch hold of her sister and hang on.

Proud Girl flew like she had never flown before, knowing that she needed to get her sister home quickly if she was to have any chance of survival. She used every ounce of her strength in the effort and was relieved when she saw the home loft in front of her.

She slowed down on approach and trapped as gently as she could.

The minute Sofi saw them, her mother's instinct kicked in. She knew this was not the time for panic and calmly instructed Proud Boy to get Joe. She cleared the nest box and lay with her daughter holding her and gently talking to her.

"My Leif, you are safe now. I have got you. You are going to be okay."

Princess Elisabeth was slipping in and out of consciousness but could hear her mother's soft voice and knew she was in a safe place.

Meanwhile, Proud Boy had flown against the scullery window to attract Joe's attention and was hovering flapping his wings furiously. When Joe appeared Proud Boy shouted,

"Come quick, Princess Elisabeth has been badly hurt and she's bleeding!"

Joe ran out to the loft and shouted to Adrian to get the medical kit. He gently inspected the young bird and saw that her craw had been sliced open. He could not see any other damage, but he knew he needed to stem the flow of blood.

He asked Adrian to give him the needle and thread from the box. "Son, I need you to hold the wound together while I stitch." He showed Adrian how to gently pinch the sides of the open cut together and began to stitch. Joe was glad he'd paid attention when watching Minnie mend the boy's clothes years earlier. It was a skill he'd put to use many times over the years with the pigeons, and he always thought gratefully of his young wife as he did.

When he had finished, Joe stepped back to inspect his handiwork and was pleased with the results. He bathed the wound using a mild antiseptic.

"I think she is going to be okay, we got to her in time," he told Sofi and Proud Boy. "She will be sore for a day or two, and we'll need to watch her temperature in case of an infection."

He turned to Adrian. "You did well, Son. Good job."

Now that things had settled, Sofi turned to her other daughter, hugged her, and cried,

"I am so proud of you. You did not leave your sister and you saved her life." Proud Girl gently kissed her mother and said, "It wasn't all down to me. If it had not been for Bootsy's quick thinking we could all have been killed. He is the real hero!"

The Young Bird Derby

Everyone was relieved that Princess Elisabeth was going to survive, but they were disappointed as well. They knew that Sofi would not allow her other daughter to race on her own. Joe, Adrian, and Proud Boy were now resigned to the fact that this would mean the season was effectively over for them and that the attempt at the elusive Derby victory would have to wait for another year.

Yet, during the night, Sofi continued to wrestle with the dilemma of letting Proud Girl go to the Derby without her sister. She knew that it was in her children's blood to race, and she knew how much it meant to Joe and Adrian, whom she had grown to love deeply. She decided she could not disappoint them.

First thing in the morning, she told Proud Boy, "Please go and tell Joe that Proud Girl can go to Penzance, but on one condition."

Proud Boy tilted his head to one side and looked at her quizzically.

"I want Bootsy to go as her minder," Sofi said firmly. "I have watched him with the girls, and I know he will do everything in his power to protect her. He has proven himself to be very clever and whilst not the quickest racer, he has great strength and stamina."

Proud Boy marvelled at the wisdom of this little lady from Belgium. He kissed her, told her he loved her, and added, "Wait till I tell Joe and Adrian! They will be delighted!"

They were indeed delighted and thought it a great plan. They arranged to have Bootsy accepted as a late substitute and then prepared to take the birds to the Club to be loaded onto the container. Proud Boy explained the situation to Bootsy, who accepted the challenge, even at such short notice.

Before Adrian came to catch the birds and put them into the basket, Proud Boy put his wing around his daughter and gently pulled her aside. He whispered some heartfelt advice to her. "Do not forget your heritage. You are a Voyageur, and you are bred for this.

"There are many great pigeons in this race, but none are as well prepared as you are. Remember that you have a strategy to cover any eventuality. Above all and no matter how hard it gets, never give up on yourself!" He paused and gave her one more bit of guidance. "Make sure you make it home safely... or your Moeke will kill me!"

They both laughed and Proud Boy gave his daughter a big hug for good luck.

As Adrian caught and put both birds into the basket, he had his little messages for them. "See you soon, wee woman!" he said to Proud Girl, hoping she would pick up on his confidence in her. And, to Bootsy, he said, "See you sometime, Slowcoach." He knew this big fella would make it home, no matter what.

The two pigeons set off with the best wishes from everyone in the loft ringing in their ears. All the talk at the Club was of Princess Elisabeth's attack. The other fanciers all wished her a speedy recovery. A few also asked if Joe fancied 'the wee hen' to do well in the race. Joe just smiled.

After all the birds from the various clubs around the country were loaded, the conveyor made its way to Larne and boarded the ferry for the crossing to the mainland. Proud Girl knew she would be flying against the best birds in the country but was not prepared for what happened next.

Some of the city birds overheard her and Bootsy chatting and started to laugh at them.

"Look at the country bumpkins! Listen to the way they talk!"

All the other birds laughed. A very large male approached and shouted in a sharp Belfast accent, "Here's me like! I am from West Belfast, and I can beat any of yey!"

He looked straight at Proud Girl and continued shouting, "Look at all the size of yey, there is no way yey will make it home!"

Again this was followed by hurtful cackling and laughter.

Bootsy had heard enough. He jumped in front of Proud Girl and shouted back. "Leave her alone! If any of you come near her, you will have me to deal with!"

As with all bullies, these Belfast boys were not used to anyone standing up to them. They immediately backed off. They just didn't fancy tangling with this angry big red Calf Lane boy.

Bootsy put his wing around Proud Girl, ushered her to a position he felt would be ideal come release time, and decided to settle there for the night. Proud Girl had never experienced such bullying and attempted intimidation in her life and was seething inside. "Just wait!" she thought to herself, "I will show you lot what a 'wee country bumpkin' can do!"

Back home, there were growing concerns as the weather forecast was turning very nasty. Adrian practically never left the radio, listening for any snippet of better news. On Saturday morning the conditions were so poor in the Penzance area that word filtered back that they were considering holding the birds back until the next day in hope of better weather. The birds in the conveyor knew things were not good and could hear the rain and feel the strong winds against the side of the vehicle.

Suddenly, things brightened up and the race organizers decided to release the birds to take advantage of the break in the weather. Before Proud Girl and Bootsy knew it, the sides of the cages dropped, and they were off. As they had positioned themselves at the front the previous evening, they managed to get away cleanly and settled into the leading batch heading north.

As their heads cleared, Proud Girl called out to Bootsy, "Let's just fly with this group for a little while and work out our strategy." Bootsy called back, "That works for me! You're the boss!"

She smiled at him, put her head down and thought of the race ahead. They were flying into a strong headwind and knew that this would be a relatively slow race that would sap their energy.

The plan they'd worked on with Proud Boy called for immediately heading out to sea aiming to hit land on the southern tip of Ireland if the wind was from the south. But as some birds were breaking off and heading for the coast, Proud Girl called out to Bootsy, "Plan B! We will keep going north before we attempt to cross." Bootsy nodded in agreement.

Plan B, again devised by Proud Boy, was if the wind was in their face, they were to fly up the coast to the familiar territory of Haverford West and cross from there to Wexford.

The Weather Worsens

As they continued north, the weather deteriorated further, making flying conditions very difficult. The leading batch was getting smaller and smaller, with some birds struggling to keep up and others dropping off. As they approached Haverford West, the sky had darkened, and visibility was very poor. Bootsy was becoming very concerned about trying to cross and called over to Proud Girl, "Keep going north, it is too dangerous to try to cross now. The wind has changed to coming from the northwest and the strength of it and the poor visibility will make it impossible!" She nodded. They ignored the others and continued north.

Soon they were facing a full-blown gale and torrential rain. The sky was now jet black, lit up only by an occasional flash of lightning. Bootsy could see that Proud Girl was visibly tiring and it was obvious that she would soon need to rest.

"Fly behind me!" he called, "I'll protect you from the wind!"

She did not have the will to argue and fell in behind him. As we know, he was not the fastest bird alive, but he was tremendously strong and made good speed whilst buffering her from the worst of the weather. She was struggling but kept repeating her Pa's words in her head. "Keep going! Focus and

fly! Do not give up on yourself! Do not give up on yourself!"
With those words echoing in her head and her confidence in
Bootsy, she was able to keep going.

When Bootsy knew they had made it to Scotland and
realised that there was no chance of crossing to Ireland in
these conditions, he started to look for somewhere to rest and
saw a little nook on the cliffs looking out toward home. He
directed Proud Girl to land there.

She was utterly exhausted and very relieved when she
heard Bootsy say, "We need to rest and take shelter here and
try to ride out the worst of the weather. We will try the
crossing in the morning."

Will It Be a Smash?

Back at home, all the fanciers were extremely worried. There were no reports of any pigeons having made it home yet. Second-guessing had begun about the decision to release the birds in such bad weather as they were now undoubtedly facing 'a smash' – the name for a heart-breaking race in which many pigeons are lost.

Joe and Adrian had remained at the scullery window, hoping against hope, until the last light disappeared from the sky. Proud Boy was in the nest box with Sofi and Princess Elisabeth, trying to hide his concern from them, but he was, by now, really worried about the safety of his daughter. Sofi was beside herself and said silent prayers all night long, wishing for the safe return of her precious Lief. Princess Elisabeth prayed too, wishing she was with her sister. She could just not imagine life without her. The only thing that reassured her was that she knew Bootsy would do everything in his power to keep her safe.

Meanwhile, Proud Girl and Bootsy, both exhausted and soaking-wet, settled into their resting place. Proud Girl was shivering uncontrollably from the cold. Bootsy wrapped his wings around her and said, "Snuggle in tight to me and try to rest. Try to sleep and we'll see how things look in the morning."

He turned his broad back to the wind and rain, forming a barrier and creating a little cocoon. Proud Girl soon felt safe and warm. Bootsy stood all night, taking a horrendous battering from the weather. As morning approached, he was stiff, sore, and freezing.

Back home, Joe did not sleep well either. But for some reason, he had a feeling that this little bird was going to make it. He got up at first light and returned to his position by the scullery window. He drank tea and chain-smoked as he watched the sky for any sign of the young bird.

Back on the cliff top, Proud Girl was stirring and feeling much better. She could see that the weather had improved and said to Bootsy, "Come on, we need to get on our way and try crossing now."

Bootsy answered her, "'If you are to have any chance of winning, you are going to have to go on from here on your own. I am freezing and will only slow you down."

It was only then that she realized that he had stood all night protecting her and was now in a pretty bad way.

Bootsy shrugged off her concerns. "You should continue north and then cross," he told her. "Remember your dad said we were to do this if things were really bad? He told us to go as far north as possible before turning for home and trying to cross the water. He said the wind would then be at our backs as we go over the water and make it easier for us."

Proud Boy had given this a lot of thought. He knew how difficult it was to win long-distance races against birds from down the country when flying to locations on the North Coast. He had tried and failed.

The only one to do so was a bird owned by Anthony McDonnell from Damhead, just outside Coleraine, called the

Bann King, which won the King's Cup from Les Sables in 1963. This remarkable pigeon flew a total of 621 miles which remains to this day the longest distance covered by any winner.

Proud Boy knew that speed and strength alone were not enough to overcome the disadvantage of having to fly further than the others. He felt the only way a bird could do it was to use bad conditions to its advantage. He imagined being able to get far enough north that the wind would turn in a bird's favour and help carry him, or in this case, her, home. Knowing that the weather was likely to be bad, he had thrown this scenario into the mix at the last minute before Proud Girl and Bootsy left for the race. Now his theory was going to be put to the test.

As Proud Girl hesitated, Bootsy said, "Go on, I will be okay!"

She reluctantly decided to do as he said and took to the wing. As she was rising into the sky, she heard him call, "Go on girl! Show them what you are made of!" Followed by the old standing joke, "See you tomorrow!"

This made her laugh and lifted her spirits. It also made her even more determined to make it home as quickly as possible. She also thought of the bullies from the night before and their cruel remarks. She said to herself, "I will show you lot!"

She continued north for a little then felt the wind change. Little by little it was more and more into her tail and whilst it was still raining, she decided to set out across the water.

Proud Girl felt strong and confident as the wind helped carry her and it was not long before she saw the familiar sight of the Giant's Causeway in the distance. She knew she had not far to go from there and this buoyed her even more. She decided to give it everything she had.

Joe had continued his vigil and had been joined by Adrian at the window. They were scanning the sky to the south, looking for any sign of the birds. Proud Boy and Warhorse were in their positions on the roof, also looking south, but with Proud Boy taking an occasional hopeful glance over his shoulder to the north.

"Do you think she can do it?" Adrian asked. "I think she will make it home," Joe said, "but if she is going to win, she will need to come soon."

He had no sooner said the words than he got the shock of his life as he saw the little warrior swoop down onto the loft. He almost jumped out of his skin, as he was not prepared for her to be coming in from behind him.

"There she is! There she is!" They shouted in unison.

Joe grabbed his mixture tin and bolted out to the loft. There was no need to worry as she had already been trapped and was pecking whatever she could find on the floor as she was so hungry. He lifted her and could hardly get the rubber race ring off her leg as his hands were shaking so much. When she was successfully clocked, an enormous roar rose out of the loft with the other birds cheering at the top of their voices and clapping their wings as loud as they could. The roar from the loft was so loud that it was heard all around the Calf Lane and all the other fanciers knew that Joe's 'wee hen' was home.

Her mother and sister rushed to her, hugged her, and gently ushered her to the quiet and safety of the nest box. Back in the nest box, they were fussing over her when in the middle of all the chaos, Princess Elisabeth asked, "What about Bootsy? Is he okay?"

Proud Girl replied, "Yes, he's fine – safe and well." And proceeded to tell them of how clever and brave he had been, sending her on her way with the message: "See you tomorrow!" They all laughed, and Sofi noticed how relieved Princess Elisabeth was to hear this news.

The rest of the day was a bit of a blur for Joe and Adrian with the other fanciers calling to see how their bird was doing and to pass on any information they had about the race.

They had to wait until later that evening for the results to be announced. They sat glued to the radio as the results were read out from the National Union of Racing Pigeon Headquarters.

The announcer confirmed that only a total of four birds out of 200 entered were clocked in race time. He then continued, "It is my great pleasure to announce the winner..."

After the obligatory dramatic pause, he said:

"Moffatt Brothers from Coleraine Premier Racing Pigeon Society."

Joe and Adrian could not believe it and broke into a joyous dance around the kitchen. (Even Frankie joined in!) Adrian ran out to the loft and shouted to Proud Girl: "You've done it! You've done it! You have only gone and won it!" Again a mighty din sounded in the loft.

The celebrations went on long into the night.

The next morning Joe rose early and took up his position at the scullery window with his tea and cigarettes. Proud Boy and Warhorse resumed their positions on the roof of the house. When Adrian rose, he immediately understood what was happening; they were all waiting for Bootsy! He realized that this race would not be over for his dad and the other birds until the last bird was home.

Bootsy did not disappoint them, but as usual, made them wait quite a while until he came lazily gliding over the rooftops to land on the traps with a tired thump. Everyone was delighted to see him, and all cheered as loud as they could. Some even broke out singing, led by Proud Boy. "For he's a jolly good fellow! For he's a jolly good fellow! For he's a jolly good fellow, and so say all of us!"

When she saw Bootsy, Princess Elisabeth flung herself at him, hugging him. "I am so glad to see you," she shouted, thumping him on his wing. "You big galloot, what kept you? I was so worried!"

She kissed him, saying, "I love you!" Bootsy was delighted to hear this. He was devoted to both sisters, but Princess Elisabeth was the one who had his heart.

Proud Girl joined them, saying, "Thank you so much, I could never have done it without you!" Bootsy whispered, "I know!" And they all laughed and danced around, hugging each other.

Sofi nudged Proud Boy. "See? I told you so! I told you our Elisabeth had an eye for him."

Proud Boy just nodded and smiled.

The next weeks were extremely busy for Joe and Adrian with fanciers coming from all over the country to see 'the wee hen that won the smash'. A few were so impressed with her that they offered Joe money to buy her. One man, from England, clearly realized the strength of the bloodline originating with Proud Boy and offered a ridiculous sum of money for him, but Joe just smiled and shook his head, politely saying, "The birds are not for sale. You see, it's not about money. These birds are family."

It took some time for things to return to normal in Maple Drive but return they did, and life went on for everyone.

Happy Endings

The birds were never sold, and Proud Boy and Sofi happily lived out the rest of their lives in the loft surrounded by several grandchildren presented to them by their girls and partners.

Proud Girl did not race again but was retired and like her father before her, was tasked with continuing the bloodline which she did very successfully.

Princess Elisabeth settled with Bootsy, the love of her life. She recovered fully from her injuries, resumed racing, and went on to get her moment in the sun, helping Joe achieve his ultimate dream, by winning the National from Avranches in France, a distance of a mere 451 miles!

This continued the family tradition for successful long-distance racing. Interestingly, this was achieved by using another strategy developed by Proud Boy to overcome the disadvantage of having to fly farther than most of the other birds. In this approach a 'peloton' concept was used, in which a team throws all its support behind the strongest member and increases their chances of winning. A unique approach, yet very appropriate for a race from the home of the Tour de France with Team Calf Lane seeing her safely home in the first place!

Joe found happiness again in his personal life when he married his second wife, Sadie, a widow, with Adrian and

Frankie gaining four stepsisters in the process: Kay, May, Margaret, and Wilma.

Adrian married his childhood sweetheart, Patricia, and moved 100 yards around the corner to live in Willow Drive where he remains to this day. They have a beautiful daughter; Andrea, son-in-law; Paul, and two grandchildren; Melissa, and Olivia. He successfully raced his team of pigeons until recently and is now involved as a volunteer organizer for the North Coast Classic one loft venture, a style of racing in which all the birds are housed in one loft and trained to race back to that location. He remains friends to this day with Big Johnnie and Wee Winky, but it must be said they never did form a C&W band!

Frankie also married his childhood sweetheart, Anne, and they had four beautiful daughters. One was sadly born asleep, then happily followed by Zara, Laura, and Ruth. All are married and with their husbands, Jonny, Gavin, and Paul, they have given Anne and Frankie five wonderful grandchildren, twins Jon and Sara, Joe, Ben, and Alex. They are the lights of their lives and are often reminded of this when Granda sings to them, "You are my sunshine!"

True to his word, Frankie has never cleaned out a pigeon loft in his life, but he did go on to play for Coleraine and he did score a goal in the Irish Cup Final. So, you see, dreams do come true!

In the years that followed, Sofi would often see Joe and Proud Boy sit together through an evening for a chat. Joe would take off his cap and put it on his knee where Proud Boy would nestle. Joe would contently light a cigarette and snuggle his pal. The love and bond they had for each other was something that she knew could never be broken nor would she ever want it to be. She realized that they had been through so much together that this was more than friendship, they were truly family.

In life, they had faced the deepest despair and the toughest challenges possible yet never gave up and came out the other side stronger and wiser. They had shared in outstanding success yet remained humble. They had raised their families the best they could and instilled in them the common courtesies of life and the values necessary to not only survive but to succeed.

She loved them both deeply and would smile when she would hear one of them begin the conversation by saying, "Did you ever imagine…?"

She knew it was time to go to bed as this was likely to be another long night of reminiscing between these two old hands.

A True Hero

And, finally, since every good tale needs a true hero, here is the story of Warhorse (or Wee Winkie as he was known as a young bird). As much as the younger birds would always come to admire him, they never knew the full extent of his heroics.

Warhorse had been one of just 32 pigeons to be awarded the Dicken Medal during the Second World War, the animal equivalent of the Victoria Cross and only given for acts of extreme heroism during the conflict.

He never talked of it, but he had been seconded to an RAF bomber unit. When the unit was returning from a mission over Norway, their Beaufort Bomber was hit by enemy fire and crashed into the sea more than 100 miles from home. Struggling in freezing waters and unable to get a radio message back to base, the four men on board faced certain death. (This was before the era of GPS and satellite locator beacons, of course.)

In a last act of desperation, the men decided to release Warhorse in the hope that he could make it back to base and help rescuers pinpoint their location. He made it, exhausted, and covered in oil, having flown 120 miles through the worst conditions imaginable.

He was not carrying a message, but the RAF were able to work out the location of the downed aircraft by calculating the time difference between the plane's ditching and the arrival of the bird, factoring in the wind direction and even the effect of the oil on Warhorse's feathers on his flight speed. A rescue mission was launched, and the men were found within 15 minutes. Warhorse became the toast of the airbase and there was a dinner held in his honour at which he was awarded his medal. It bore a simple inscription:

We Also Serve

This story only came to light many years later when he passed away and the Royal British Legion approached Joe as they wanted to bury him with full military honours. This duly happened and he was laid to rest beside the loft he had guarded all those years.

Joe had the following words put on a wooden cross:

Warhorse

A brave bird who faithfully served this loft and all who lived in it.

THE END